LONDON STEAM

D1430343

Scenes from the Fifties and Sixties

MICHAEL WELCH

Capital Transport

CONTENTS

Front cover A B1 Class 4-6-0, No. 61378, emerges from the gloomy interior of Liverpool Street Station with an unidentified van train in May 1962. The Great Eastern Railway's original London terminus was at Shoreditch, which was not only remote from the City of London, but was also unable to cope with rapidly increasing traffic. In 1865 the GER obtained an Act to construct a very costly extension to Liverpool Street, which eventually opened to suburban traffic on 2nd February 1874, and to all traffic on 1st November 1875, from which date Shoreditch was closed to passengers. The old Shoreditch terminus, latterly known as Bishopsgate, became a goods station until it was destroyed by fire in 1964. The train is leaving the older part of Liverpool Street, which was commonly known as the 'West Side' and contained Platform Nos 1 to 10. The 'East Side' of the station, which had eight platforms, was a later addition and opened on 2nd April 1894. *Roy Hobbs*

Back cover The Clapham Junction to Kensington Olympia Post Office trains remained steam hauled until the very end of steam on the South Western Division, and offered enthusiasts a welcome diversion from Bulleid 'Pacific'-hauled journeys along the Bournemouth Line. The motive power used towards the end – generally BR Standard or LMSR-designed Ivatt 2-6-2T tank engines – was also different, so this rather curious service gained an increasingly high profile as the end of SR steam loomed, and was frequently referred to as 'England's last steam branch'. This was, of course, not strictly true, but the route did have something of a branch line flavour. This was enhanced by the employment of mostly non-corridor rolling stock, including the experimental fibre-glass bodied vehicle No. S1000S. During the last week of SR steam, Ivatt Class 2MT 2-6-2T No. 41319 was a regular performer on the Kensington service, but the final train from there was taken by BR Standard 2-6-2T No. 82019 on 7th July 1967. This locomotive is seen at Kensington on 3rd May 1966, awaiting departure with the 5.36pm to Clapham Junction. *Mike Hudson*

Overleaf The rooftops and chimneys of south London provide the background to this appealing shot of 'Schools' Class 4-4-0 No. 30911 *Dover* approaching Honor Oak Park Station at the head of the 5.25pm London Bridge to Reading and Tonbridge train. Note the familiar telegraph poles, which are now rarely seen on railway routes – just one of so many changes which have occurred over the years since this picture was taken in June 1962. *Colin Hogg*

First Published 1999

ISBN 1 85414 214 3

Published by Capital Transport Publishing
38 Long Elmes, Harrow Weald, Middlesex

Printed by CS Graphics, Singapore

INTRODUCTION

On Sunday 9th July 1967, at approximately 6.24pm, 'Merchant Navy' Pacific No. 35030 *Elder Dempster Lines*, unceremoniously reversed out of Waterloo Station and retired to Nine Elms shed. No. 35030 had doubtless followed this routine many times during its working life, but on this occasion *Elder Dempster Lines* would not see active use again. Its fire would be dropped for the last time, its remaining life left to drain away, and it would join the ranks of its lifeless brethren. On that fateful night an eerie silence descended upon the usually busy Nine Elms shed. After more than 130 glorious years, London had run out of steam and working main line steam locomotives would no longer be part of the Capital's rich heritage.

Apart from a brief period at the very beginning of the steam age, London always occupied a dominant position as the most absorbing steam centre in Great Britain. Most major routes radiated from the Capital, many prestigious express trains served it, and almost all of the busiest commuter lines were located in London. Hundreds of coal trains ran each week in order to keep the Capital's fires burning. The manner in which the railway system developed also ensured that, even as late as the 1950s, London was a Mecca for the enthusiast, offering an incredible hodge-podge of steam motive power designed by a multiplicity of railway companies and constructed by a wide range of builders. The sheer variety was astonishing, almost unbelievable. There were gleaming Class A4 Pacifics at Kings Cross, lumbering LM&SR Beyer-Garratts at Cricklewood, dignified 'Kings' at Paddington, and in contrast diminutive SE&CR P Class 0-6-0Ts fussing about at Stewarts Lane shed on pilot duty.

My own experiences of London steam were largely confined to day drips from my Sussex home in the late 1950s and 1960s. I was immediately impressed, perhaps even overwhelmed at times, by the scale of steam activity in the Capital which was so much greater than that in my adopted county, where the principal routes had long since succumbed to electrification. I particularly remember the thrill of gaining unofficial entry into the huge Stratford shed, which was hidden away amidst a vast maze of lines, on a quiet Sunday morning in the early 1960s. I had never seen a shed as large as Stratford before and, as far as I can recall, I was never challenged by the shed staff, who had probably grown tired of ejecting unauthorised visitors. Perhaps London's supreme position as a steam centre can be best gauged by comparing it with Manchester, arguably Britain's second city and a leading railway centre from the earliest days of railways. In 1937 Stratford shed alone is reputed to have had an enormous allocation of 492 locomotives, while at the same period Manchester's entire stock hovered around a paltry 1,000 engines.

During my expeditions to the Capital I often visited King's Cross, an echoing vault of a station which had a special magic for me. There was always a sense of drama and excitement when the empty stock of a famous express to the north appeared behind a humble tank engine. The spotters on the platform end would be gripped by eager anticipation, and predictions would abound regarding the identity of the main line engine which would take the train northwards. A few minutes later a locomotive, running tender first, would slowly emerge from the depths of Gasworks Tunnel. A corridor tender would immediately identify a 'Streak', as the A4 class was commonly known. Usually the spotters were disappointed when a regular sighting such as No. 60003 *Andrew K. McCosh* or No. 60028 *Walter K. Whigham* appeared, but very occasionally a 'rare' engine, perhaps running-in from Doncaster Works might unexpectedly turn up, and invariably produce spontaneous celebration amongst those who had not seen that particular engine before, which would be, of course, another precious 'cop' to be underlined in their 'ABC' book! After a few minutes the engine would be coupled on to its train, and the fireman could be seen hard at work, building up the fire in preparation for the almost twelve miles of continuous climbing out of London which lay ahead. Sometimes the locomotive would blow off unpredictably, deafening anyone unfortunate enough to be close by, and completely drowning vital station announcements. The distant sound of the guard's whistle would herald departure time, and suddenly the engine would erupt into life, perhaps engulfing unsuspecting bystanders in smoke and steam before slowly disappearing into Gasworks Tunnel at little more than walking pace. What a wonderful spectacle, which will never be forgotten!

In this album I have attempted to compile a balanced selection of pictures, within the confines of the available material, which I hope conveys at least some of the atmosphere and character of steam operation in London during the BR era. Perhaps understandably, most photographers at that time tender to favour the main routes out of the capital, so consequently colour shots of 'Jinties' on cross-London freights and suchlike eluded me! Finally, I would like to thank the many photographers who have kindly made their unique and irreplaceable slides available for publication in this album, and also express my gratitude to Terence A. Barry, David J. Fakes and Graham Mallinson, who scrutinised the original draft and suggested many worthwhile improvements.

Burgess Hill, February 1999   Michael Welch

Unlike other London termini where the last steam departure slipped out unnoticed and unrecorded, the final timetabled steam working from Paddington was well publicised in advance. Consequently, virtually every enthusiast with the slightest interest in WR steam was present when No. 7029 *Clun Castle* pulled out with the 4.15pm to Banbury on 11th June 1965. In addition many more spectators lined the route, or travelled on the train which doubtless had the atmosphere of a railtour, rather than a normal scheduled service conveying ordinary passengers. In this portrait *Clun Castle* is seen waiting to leave Paddington on that fateful day. By this time, WR steam traction was in its death throes; the number of 'Castle' Class locomotives nominally in service was down to four, and one of those was stored out of use at Gloucester. At the end of June, however, three of the remaining engines were withdrawn, leaving only No. 7029, which had become the flagship of WR steam, in traffic. A fair number of ex-GWR steam engines remained in service particularly at Oxford, Worcester and in the West Midlands, but most were in decrepit condition and destined for withdrawal before the end of 1965. The last ex-GWR steam locomotives were withdrawn from Tyseley shed, Birmingham, in November 1966. *Paul Leavens*

WESTERN REGION LINES

Photographs of gleaming 'King' and 'Castle' Class locomotives leaving Paddington at the head of expresses are relatively commonplace, but shots of humble pannier tank engines entering the station hauling empty stock workings are, perhaps, much rarer. In this picture, taken on 5th April 1964, WR 5700 Class 0-6-0PT No. 4615 is seen approaching the station in charge of a long rake of empty coaches. The locomotive appears to be expending considerable effort in its attempt to keep the train on the move. This class totalled more than eight hundred engines, numerically one of the largest classes operated in Great Britain. This picture offers an excellent view of the comparatively uncongested approach to Paddington Station. *Mike Hudson*

Class 1500 0-6-0PT No. 1500 is pictured at Royal Oak, just outside Paddington Station, on empty stock duties, on 19th October 1963. This machine was one of a batch of ten GWR-designed heavy-duty pannier tank engines which emerged from Swindon Works between May and September 1949. They were designed by F.W. Hawksworth, who made a radical departure from the usual Swindon tradition for pannier tanks, by incorporating outside cylinders and Walschaerts valve gear, which gave them an ungainly appearance. They had a very short wheelbase which enabled them to negotiate sharp curves, but precluded their use at high speed. The class will probably be best remembered for its use on empty stock trains to and from Paddington, a small batch being allocated to Old Oak Common shed specifically for this purpose. In addition, some representatives of the class were also shedded in South Wales. Fortunately, following displacement from their Paddington empty stock duties, three examples were purchased for further use by the National Coal Board. They visited Barclay's works at Kilmarnock (!) for overhaul, and repainting in maroon livery, prior to taking up residence at Coventry colliery. One engine was later purchased by the Warwickshire Railway Society and survives in preservation at the Severn Valley Railway. It returned to steam in 1998 after a lengthy overhaul. *R.C. Riley*

5

By the end of the 1920s there was a growing need to replace the hundreds of old saddle and pannier tank locomotives which were in use throughout the GWR system. No. 5700 appeared from North British Locomotive Works in 1929, and became a forerunner of a class which eventually totalled 863 engines. Construction of the class was undertaken by seven different builders, including Swindon Works, of course, and spanned a period of 21 years. The excellence of the design was recognised by London Transport which purchased a small batch for use on engineers' trains, and some of these engines remained in traffic until 1971, by which time they had become the last steam engines in regular use in the London area. They were extremely successful machines, being very powerful for their size, free running and able to accelerate swiftly. No. 9704, seen here at Subway Junction on 19th October 1963, was one of ten locomotives fitted with condensing apparatus for working over the Metropolitan Widened Lines. They were always based at Old Oak Common Shed. *R.C. Riley*

An up express from South Wales to London, hauled by a gleaming 'Castle' Class 4-6-0 No. 4094 *Dynevor Castle*, passes Old Oak Common on 13th August 1960, while an up empty stock working approaches on the viaduct above the main line. Note the incredibly varied selection of coaches assembled in the train. The first three vehicles immediately behind the engine are of BR Standard design, and display three different liveries: maroon, carmine & cream and chocolate & cream. Coaches painted in the last-mentioned colours were normally restricted to use on selected named WR expresses at that time. The fourth vehicle appears to be a restaurant car of GWR design, behind which is a GWR-designed compartment coach. *R.C. Riley*

On the last stage of its journey to London, 'Castle' Class No. 7034 *Ince Castle*, in rather scruffy condition by WR standards, passes West London Junction (which is just out of sight beyond the bridge) with the up 'Cheltenham Spa Express' on 29th September 1962. Trains from the WR could gain access to the Willesden to Clapham Junction line at West London Junction, and proceed to destinations on the SR. By this time coaches in carmine and cream livery were rapidly being repainted in maroon, which had been generally adopted as the standard livery for locomotive-hauled stock, apart from the SR which largely retained traditional green. The nearer of the two girder bridges in the background carries a roadway across the railway, while the other bridge takes trains on the Willesden to Clapham Junction route across the Great Western main line. *Paul Leavens*

A down local train, formed of BR Standard compartment stock and hauled by 61XX Class 2-6-2T No. 6120, leaves West Ealing on 1st June 1957. The GWR signal box and semaphore signals, not to mention the row of trees along the roadway adjoining the line and distant station buildings, made this an appealing setting for photography. The line to Greenford can be seen diverging on the left of the picture. Note the shiny tracks into the goods yard, which was obviously still very much in use at this time. The 61XX Class, which numbered 70 engines, was designed by Collett and introduced in the early 1930s specifically for London suburban services. Virtually the entire class was based in the London (Old Oak Common) motive power district, which included sheds as distant from the Capital as Reading and Didcot. Members of this class were a familiar sight on suburban trains to and from Paddington until they were replaced by diesel multiple units as part of the BR Modernisation Plan. *R.C. Riley*

Many photographs of down trains approaching Southall, taken from a bridge east of the station with the motive power depot on the right of the shot, have been published over the years, but views looking west from the same vantage point are scarcer. This scene of Southall Station was taken on 10th August 1957, and shows the up 'Mayflower' express from Plymouth, which is apparently about to stop at the signal, which has obstinately refused to clear. In addition to the signal, other everyday items of station 'furniture' include the water cranes and braziers (known colloquially as 'fire devils'), plus the familiar gas lamps. Naturally the station is kitted out with 'sausage' signs and nameboards in the regional colours. Note the train's formation which is massive by today's standards, though it must be admitted that more frequent services operate nowadays than in steam days. An unidentified WR 2-6-2T locomotive can just be discerned simmering in the parcels bay between duties. Motive power was provided by 'King' Class 4-6-0 No. 6027 *King Richard I*, which was built at Swindon Works in July 1930 and remained in traffic until September 1962. *R.C. Riley*

A begrimed 'County' Class 4-6-0 No. 1014 *County of Glamorgan* is seen approaching Iver with a Paddington to Weston-super-Mare relief train on 13th August 1960. The 'County' Class was designed by F. W. Hawksworth, who was the GWR's Chief Mechanical Engineer from July 1941 to 1946. The class first appeared in August 1945 and represented a break with GWR tradition. The main new features were a double blastpipe, a non-standard coupled wheel diameter of 6ft 3ins and a high boiler pressure of 280lbs. The class also had a high axle loading which resulted in speed restrictions being imposed over many routes. In addition, its heavy 'hammer blow' could have been the reason why construction of the class was restricted to only 30 examples. *C. Hogg*

The busiest route from Paddington was the main line to the west through Reading and consequently the Paddington to Birmingham line via High Wycombe tended to be overlooked by photographers. Amongst the few transparencies of this route submitted for publication was this pleasing portrait of 'King' Class No. 6022 *King Edward III* approaching West Ruislip with the 8.55am Birkenhead Woodside to Paddington train on 14th May 1960. The 'Kings' had a highly unusual front bogie design, which incorporated outside bearings for the leading axle, and inside for the trailing axle. Note that the train is formed of carriages in both old and new BR liveries, the vehicle immediately behind the locomotive being a BR Standard Full Brake Van, a type which was known in railway parlance as a BG. West Ruislip was an interesting location, which had a set of watertroughs north of the station. Today, it is one of the Central Line's west London terminal stations, but if London Transport's plans had come to fruition in the 1930s, the line would have been extended to Denham. *C. Hogg*

THE GREAT CENTRAL LINE

Marylebone Station, opened in 1899, was the terminus of the Great Central Railway's London extension, which was the last main line to enter London. It was a very modest terminus, consisting of only four platforms and possessed a distinctly provincial flavour. The line's promoters optimistically acquired a large area of land to permit future expansion of the station, but this was never needed, because the GCR was a commercial failure from the start. In all, some fifty-one acres of land were purchased for development of the passenger terminus, goods and coal depots, and some of London's worst tenements were demolished by the GCR to provide space. The GCR's chairman, Sir Edward Watkin, had to overcome opposition from the wealthy and influential residents of St John's Wood, and members of the Marylebone Cricket Club at Lord's. One of the most distinctive features of Marylebone was the large, and very attractive porte-cochère of iron and glass which spanned the roadway between the station and the adjoining, massive Hotel Great Central, which completely dwarfed the station. The hotel later became the headquarters of the British Transport Commission and subsequently the British Railways Board, and was unimaginatively known as '222 Marylebone Road'. In this view, taken early on the morning of Saturday 18th August 1962, a clean LMSR Class 5MT 4-6-0 No. 44814 is seen at the buffer stops after arrival with an overnight cheap fare, 'Starlight Special' from Glasgow.
Geoff Rixon

On the glorious afternoon of 2nd September 1966, the penultimate day of through GCR route services, 'Black Five' No. 44872 has just passed under Rossmore Road bridge on the first stage of its journey northwards with the 4.38pm semi-fast train from Marylebone to Nottingham Victoria. It will shortly enter the first of a series of tunnels and covered ways which take the line under the Lord's cricket ground and the streets of fashionable St John's Wood. By the date of this photograph, main line services along the GCR route had been reduced to only three semi-fast trains a day. When the line opened, there were eleven trains each way on weekdays, seven of them expresses to and from Manchester, and through services were also provided to such far-flung destinations as Stratford-on-Avon and Bradford. The GCR found it difficult to attract traffic from its longer established rivals, however, its journey time to Manchester, for example, being much longer than the competing LNWR route. By the year 1958 the number of main line arrivals at Marylebone was only eight per day and five down Manchester trains were reputedly carrying only 79 passengers apiece. *Roy Hobbs*

In 1958 the Great Central line was transferred from the ER to the LMR, which proved to be the beginning of the end of the GC Line as a through route from London to the north. Undoubtedly, the GC route was brilliantly engineered, but south of Rugby it traversed a sparsely populated area and its trains were not as well patronised as those on competing routes. Once under the jurisdiction of the LMR the writing was on the wall for the GC Line, and an almost immediate run-down of services began, the first victims being the through expresses to Sheffield and beyond which were withdrawn from 2nd January 1960. Thereafter a token service of three daily semi-fast trains was provided between Marylebone and Nottingham Victoria. Unfortunately, the LMR operating authorities gave the doomed GC route's motive power requirements the lowest priority, and many locomotives working out their mileage prior to withdrawal were drafted to the line. This deliberate policy had a disastrous effect on timekeeping as failures abounded and helped to drive away the few passengers who remained loyal to the line. In this view a filthy 'Royal Scot' No. 46126 *Royal Army Service Corps* is seen near Kilburn on the last stage of its journey to the Capital, with the 8.15am Nottingham to Marylebone on 25th May 1963. No. 46126 was withdrawn five months after this picture was taken. *Michael Allen*

For many years Rickmansworth was the traditional engine changing point for London Transport Metropolitan Line services between Baker Street and Aylesbury. These were hauled by electric locomotives as far as Rickmansworth, where steam traction took over for the remainder of the run. In this picture, former Metropolitan Railway electric locomotive No.1 *John Lyon*, which is just visible in the background, had just been detached from a northbound train, and Thompson L1 2-6-4T No.67788 is seen coming on to the train, prior to departure to Aylesbury. Note the delightful wooden bodied coach, part of which can be seen on the right of the shot. These 'Dreadnought' vehicles were introduced in 1909/10 and further batches were built up to 1923. Great changes took place in this area in September 1960 when services from Baker Street to Amersham and Chesham were electrified. A year later, on 9th September 1961, Metropolitan trains from Amersham to Aylesbury were replaced by a LMR service from Marylebone, the final Metropolitan train from Aylesbury to Amersham being hauled by LMSR 2-6-4T No.42230. *Neil Davenport*

This charming image of vintage steam at Chesham Station depicts a former Great Central Railway 4-4-2T No. 67418 awaiting departure with a train to Chalfont and Latimer. This splendid picture was taken on 27th March 1954, before colour photography became commonplace. The station buildings, on the left, appear to be rather dilapidated, but at least the signalbox brightens up the scene. Note the array of colourful advertisements for Nescafé coffee, Walls ice cream and the latest pictures showing at the Regent Cinema, Amersham. No. 67418 was a product of Gorton Works, Manchester, and was built in September 1903: the class numbered 40 locomotives. During its long career it carried various numbers, its first being GCR No. 193. It was initially numbered 5193 by the LNER, but this was later altered to 7418. The engine was withdrawn from service in December 1958. *Neil Davenport*

A view of Wembley Hill Station on Cup Final Day, 25th May 1963, as 'Black Five' No. 45062 pulls away from the up platform with the empty stock of the 12.20pm arrival from Loughborough Central which conveyed Leicester City supporters to the match. The train appears to be comprised mainly of LMSR-designed stock, but also includes a BR Standard catering vehicle. This train would presumably have been routed down the GC Line as far as Grendon Underwood Junction, from where it would have gained the GW&GC Joint Line to reach Wembley Hill. A number of football specials from the East Midlands also travelled down the Midland Line to St Pancras, but it is recorded that the majority of those were diesel-hauled, much to the dismay of lineside photographers who were expecting a large number of steam workings. Unfortunately, the fans who came down on this train would have returned disappointed, because their team was convincingly defeated by Manchester United. *Michael Allen*

The GCR's exit from London, sharing the tracks of the Metropolitan Railway for much of the way, was not ideal and it was not unknown for delays to be caused by the Metropolitan's stopping services. The route was also heavily graded, with a stiff climb, mostly in tunnel, out of Marylebone. This was followed by another ascent of almost three miles from Neasden to Harrow-on-the-Hill, which included a section graded at 1 in 91. The line later climbed again, mostly at 1 in 105, all of the way from Watford South Junction to Amersham. There were also severe curves at Rickmansworth and Aylesbury which prevented much fast running. The GWR's proposed new line from Paddington to Birmingham via High Wycombe soon aroused the interest of the GCR and the two companies reached agreement regarding a shared section, which was to be operated by a joint committee, and opened in April 1906. The disadvantage of the extra mileage was more than outweighed by the new route's easier grades and reduced traffic occupation compared to the Metropolitan Line. Two link lines were built from the existing GCR line, and the southerly one connected Neasden and Northolt. In this scene, recorded on 24th January 1954, a down express headed by B1 Class 4-6-0 No. 61001 *Eland* is depicted passing through Northolt Park Station on the above section of line. *Neil Davenport*

THE WEST COAST LINE

The reconstruction of Euston was well under way by the time this scene was recorded on 31st July 1964. LMSR 'Jubilee' 6P5F Class No. 45672 *Anson*, which is in quite clean condition, simmers at the buffer stops having just arrived with the 9.05am train from Llandudno. The photographer states that the train was electrically hauled from Crewe to Nuneaton, which was apparently the limit of electric working at that time. Presumably the train was steam hauled from Llandudno to Crewe so the journey, which included two engine changes, was certainly interesting! Note the LNER Gresley-designed coach which looks rather out of place at Euston.
Neville Simms

In the early 1960s a fascinating mixture of steam and diesel hauled trains, together with electrics on local services to Watford, could be found at Euston. In this picture, LMSR 'Princess Coronation' Pacific No. 46246 *City of Manchester* stands in Platform 2 after arrival with a train from Liverpool, sometime in 1961. An English Electric Type 4 diesel locomotive (later Class 40) sits in Platform 1, after apparently having just arrived on another express from the north. Euston, London's first main-line station, was opened on 20th July 1837 and was famous for the impressive Doric Arch, built to commemorate the confident new age of the railway, and the magnificent Great Hall, which was opened in 1849. The rest of the station was constructed piecemeal over a sixty-year period however, and was hardly a worthy London terminus for the self-styled 'Premier Line'. In 1935 the LMSR proposed to raze the whole place to the ground, and in 1938 the Company's Chairman dramatically threw a switch in the shareholders' meeting room at Euston which blasted 100,000 tons of limestone at Caldon Low (Staffordshire) quarries to build the new station. Alas, it was not to be, because the Second World War intervened. Despite protests, the entire station was rebuilt in the early 1960s in preparation for the electrification from London to Manchester and Liverpool. *T.J. Edgington*

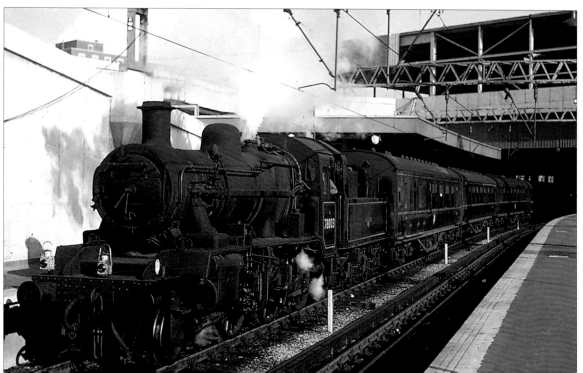

BR Standard Class 2MT No. 78003 shunts empty coaching stock at the 'country end' of Euston Station in May 1965. In the background the new, rather soulless, terminus takes shape. At this time the remaining steam engines employed in the Euston area, based at Willesden shed, were confined to mundane duties such as that seen here, the only main line work being on freight rosters. When Willesden shed closed its doors four months later, steam traction ended at Euston after nearly 130 years. *J.G. Dewing*

When the site for the London & Birmingham Railway's terminus was being considered in the 1830s, various locations were put forward including Marble Arch and Maiden Lane, near Kings Cross. In 1833 a terminus was authorised at Camden Town, but in the following year the directors decided to venture a little nearer London, and agreed on the site at Euston Grove. This extension involved crossing the Regent's Canal which created a fairly severe 1 in 68/1 in 77 gradient from the platform ends at Euston, and for a time the section between Euston and Camden was cable-worked. In steam days, Camden Bank was a formidable test for locomotives starting from cold at Euston Station, and banking assistance was often used for the initial stage of the climb. In this July 1963 picture, Stanier 'Black Five' No. 45000 is seen tackling the bank in fine style, apparently with steam to spare. No. 45000 was one of the earliest members of its class to be built, emerging from Crewe Works in February 1935. It remained in traffic until October 1967 and is now preserved as part of the National Collection. *J.G. Dewing*

An immaculately turned-out Fowler 2-6-4T No. 42350 passes Camden No. 1 signal box with a northbound train of empty coaches on 14th June 1962. The photographer comments that this engine was the 'Pride of Willesden' at this time, which doubtless accounts for its polished condition. *J.G. Dewing*

A scene at the west end of Kensal Green Tunnel, on a sunny 4th August 1962, as LMSR 'Patriot' Class 7P 4-6-0 No. 45530 *Sir Frank Ree* emerges at the head of a train from Euston to Barrow-in-Furness/Whitehaven. In those days more places enjoyed the benefits of through services to and from the Capital and trains were often made up of various portions, which were 'split' *en route*. In this case it is likely that the train was divided at Barrow, from where the front portion continued along the coast of Cumberland to Whitehaven Bransty. From South Hampstead to Kensal Green Station the West Coast Main Line runs in a south-westerly direction, but here is running more or less due west, prior to turning in a north-westerly direction at Willesden Junction, just over a mile from this point. No. 45530 is an interesting locomotive; it was originally built to the design of Henry Fowler in 1933, but in October 1946 was rebuilt by H.G. Ivatt with a 2A type boiler, new cylinders and a double chimney. It later became the final survivor of its class, lasting in service until December 1965. *Paul Leavens*

Coverage of the West Coast Main Line would not be complete without a view of Willesden shed, especially if the shot is enhanced by two of Sir William Stanier's 'Princess Coronation' class Pacifics – surely the most magnificent steam locomotives ever to run in Great Britain. A shed first appeared on this site in 1873 and was enlarged in 1898. In 1929 a large roundhouse was completed which gained brief fame in 1954 as a display gallery during the International Railway Congress. In 1960 a total of 130 engines was based at the depot, principally for parcels, freight and empty stock movements. Willesden motive power depot lacked the glamour of Camden shed, just outside Euston Station, which had a fleet of express passenger engines, but was by far the larger of the two. When Camden was closed in September 1963, a little of the glamour rubbed off on Willesden however, when the former depot's last remaining Pacifics, Nos 46239/40/45, were transferred there. In this picture, taken on 8th June 1964, Nos 46239 *City of Chester* (nearest to the camera) and 46245 *City of London* can be seen, with a rather dirty 'Jubilee' 4-6-0 No. 45676 *Codrington* on the extreme right of the shot. Willesden shed closed in September 1965 and the site is now occupied by a Freightliner depot. *Paul Leavens*

The Class 9F 2-10-0s were widely acknowledged to be the most successful of the BR Standard types. Designed principally for heavy freight haulage, they sometimes appeared on passenger trains when they performed excellently and proved capable of a fair turn of speed. In the early 1960s some were transferred to the Somerset & Dorset Line for working heavy passenger trains, where their prodigious haulage capacity eliminated the need to double-head the heavier trains. Sadly, the working lives of these modern and competent locomotives were curtailed by the widespread introduction of diesels under the BR Modernisation Plan. In the London area, the Class 9Fs could be seen on most main routes north of the River Thames, and were especially common on the Midland main line where they hauled coal traffic from the East Midlands to the Capital, work which was previously undertaken by the LMSR Beyer-Garratts. Here, No. 92102 is seen charging along the West Coast main line near Kenton with a northbound train of iron ore empties sometime in the late 1950s. *The late Derek Cross*

The rooftops and chimneys of north-west London form the backdrop as the up 'Caledonian' express whisks through Kenton almost at the end of its 400-miles long journey from Glasgow to London. Motive power is provided by 'Princess Coronation' Pacific No. 46225 *Duchess of Gloucester*, and this shot is thought to have been taken in about 1959. At that time the 'Caledonian' was booked to leave Glasgow at 8.30am and arrive at London Euston at 3.45pm. Due to its tight schedule, the train was limited to eight coaches, including a restaurant car. Note the train's distinctive headboard and the formation, which includes some LMSR coaches in addition to BR Standard vehicles which make up the bulk of the set. *The late Derek Cross*

A breathtaking portrait of a down express, bathed in glorious low winter sunlight, near Headstone Lane on 20th February 1954. Note the LMSR coaches in the distinctive carmine and cream livery of that period. The local passenger lines on the right were used by London Transport and BR Euston to Watford services. The slow line tracks are almost hidden behind the train on the left of the picture. Motive power was provided by 'Princess Coronation' Class Pacific No. 46246 *City of Manchester* which was constructed at Crewe in August 1943. It ran for a short period as a streamlined engine, but the casing was removed in September 1946. In February 1949 it was painted in experimental BR black livery and was painted green in June 1954. A further livery change occurred in October 1958 when *City of Manchester* was turned out in maroon livery. In January 1963 it became one of the first of its class to be condemned. *Neil Davenport*

In this wonderfully evocative picture, 'Royal Scot' 4-6-0 No.46126 *Royal Army Service Corps* is depicted passing through Hatch End Station at the head of the up 'Ulster Express' on Sunday, 11th April 1954. Note the bullhead track, on which the train is travelling, semaphore signalling, vintage LMSR station nameboard and crimson and cream coaching stock – how different the railway scene was in those days. In the 1959 timetable, 'The Ulster Express' connected with the 9.40pm overnight steamer from Belfast to Heysham Harbour, from where it departed to London Euston via Birmingham at 6.55am. On Sundays the advertised arrival time at Euston was at 1.30pm, giving a truly marathon journey which few people would relish today. Regrettably, No. 46126 ended its working life in neglected condition working Marylebone to Nottingham semi-fast trains during the dying days of the Great Central route, and is pictured on one of these trains elsewhere in this album. *Neil Davenport*

STEAM FROM MOORGATE

A through service of local trains operated to Moorgate from suburban stations north of St Pancras for many years, for the benefit of city workers, and indeed the first trains along the Midland Line south of Bedford, in July 1868, terminated there because St Pancras was not ready. In this fascinating view, LMSR 2-6-2T No. 40022 is seen leaving Moorgate with the 5.11pm train to St Albans on 14th May 1959. No. 40022, which was fitted with condensing apparatus for working to Moorgate, was one of 70 engines designed by Fowler and constructed at Derby Works between 1930 and 1932. It was built in January 1931 and survived to become the final member of its class in service, not being withdrawn until December 1962. A large number of these locomotives were based in the London area for use on suburban services, until displaced by the introduction of diesel units. The electric trains on the left of the shot are Metropolitan compartment units, classified as 'T Stock'. All of these had disappeared by October 1962. *R.C. Riley*

27

THE MIDLAND LINE

In steam days the interior of St Pancras Station was rather gloomy and this, combined with unremarkable motive power, probably deterred photographers during the BR steam era. In this view, which shows 'Royal Scot' Class 4-6-0 No. 46117 *Welsh Guardsman* waiting to leave with the down 'Robin Hood' express to Nottingham in 1961, at least some of the massive roof is visible. *Colour-Rail*

The LMSR 'Jubilee' 4-6-0s were associated with express services along the Midland Main Line for many years and in this evocative scene, taken on a snowy night in January 1960, No. 45557 *New Brunswick* awaits departure with a train for Derby. The bright lights of the signal box, which replaced three mechanical boxes in 1957, are visible above the engine on the left of the picture. *J.B. Snell/Colour-Rail*

A St Pancras to Bedford local train, hauled by LMSR Class 5MT No. 44984, is seen accelerating away from Elstree Station on an August afternoon in 1959. Steam traction became a thing of the past on these workings when diesel multiple units took over, not long after this picture was taken. Today however, stopping services are provided by 'Thameslink' electric units and most run through from Brighton via Blackfriars. *The late Derek Cross*

A classic mid-1950s image of a Midland Main Line express heading northwards, in superb winter lighting conditions, just north of Elstree Station, on 20th December 1953. Motive power was provided by LMSR 'Jubilee' 4-6-0 No. 45627 *Sierra Leone*, which at that time was based at Kentish Town shed, and the train appears to be formed entirely of LMSR coaching stock in carmine and cream livery. No. 45627 emerged from Crewe Works in November 1934 and remained in service until September 1966, thus becoming one of the last members of its class in traffic. *Neil Davenport*

The record-breaking Class A4 Pacific No. 60022 *Mallard* is pictured inside Kings Cross Station in April 1963, shortly before its withdrawal from service. Kings Cross Station was largely designed by Lewis Cubitt, brother of Thomas Cubitt who founded the famous building firm. It was opened on 14th October 1852 and replaced a temporary terminus at Maiden Lane. Cubitt designed a straightforward and uncomplicated building which consisted of two 800 feet long train sheds, which were joined down the middle of the station by a brick wall carried on abutments. The passenger amenities were located on the western side of the station adjacent to one of the principal departure platforms. *Geoff Rixon*

THE EAST COAST LINE

Class A3 Pacific No. 60062 *Minoru* rests at the buffer stops at Kings Cross after arrival with a train from the north, sometime during June 1963. This was the last month of booked steam operation at Kings Cross and steam working officially became a thing of the past from June 15th, when the summer timetable started. In reality however, the operating authorities had not bargained for the appalling unreliability of the diesel fleet, and sporadic steam working continued for many months afterwards. Despite an official ban, isolated steam incursions along the Great Northern Main Line south of Peterborough lasted almost until the end of the following year, one of the last recorded workings being that of sister engine No. 60112 *St Simon*, which powered an empty stock train as far as Hornsey in November 1964. No. 60062 was built at Doncaster Works as a Class A1 locomotive in May 1925 and rebuilt to A3 Class in June 1944. It was fitted with trough smoke deflectors in July 1961, and became one of the last active members of its class, not being withdrawn until December 1964. *T.J. Edgington*

A spectacular smoke effect erupts from the chimney of A4 Class No. 60010 *Dominion of Canada* as it leaves with a train to Leeds in March 1963. When steam traction was officially banished from the southern end of the GN Main Line three months later, No. 60010 was one of eleven Class A4s moved from Kings Cross shed to Peterborough, where the engines were based for the duration of the summer timetable. In October 1963, some of its sister locomotives shedded at Peterborough were condemned, but *Dominion of Canada* was one of those engines fortunate enough to be transferred to Aberdeen (Ferryhill) shed on the Scottish Region, and given a new lease of life on the three-hour trains to Glasgow. It survived until May 1965, when it was withdrawn and subsequently preserved in Canada. *Roy Hobbs*

Kings Cross 'Top Shed' motive power depot was arguably the most famous London shed and will be best remembered by steam enthusiasts as home to many of Gresley's legendary A4 Class Pacifics. The first shed (often referred to as the 'Engine Stables') was a distinctive building with a frontage shaped like a shallow curve; it was built by the GNR in 1850/51 and consisted of 25 roads. In February 1858, the MR commenced through running of their passenger trains into Kings Cross, before the construction of their own line into St Pancras, and a roundhouse was built in 1858/59 for their use. It was situated close to the GNR's shed and was taken over by the GNR when the MR vacated their premises in 1868. In the meantime, the existing GNR shed was becoming inadequate for the increasing number of engines working into Kings Cross so, in 1862, the GNR built a new eight-road running shed. In 1929 the LNER announced the renewal of the locomotive facilities and in the early 1930s much work was undertaken, including construction of a new coaling plant and new water softening plant, an additional wheel drop, plus the installation of a 70ft turntable. The old MR roundhouse was demolished in 1931. Despite the much-heralded improvements, the original GNR shed buildings were retained, and survived largely intact until the end of steam, although it should be noted that the running shed's roof was extensively repaired in 1949. In 1958 the shed's allocation totalled 125 locomotives, including nineteen A4 Pacifics, but almost half of the engines based there were N2 Class suburban tank engines. On the occasion of the marriage of the Duke and Duchess of Kent at York in June 1961, it was decided to use steam traction to haul the Royal Train and two other trains for invited guests. Kings Cross shed provided four A4s, including a 'stand-by' locomotive, for these specials, the main train being powered by No.60028 *Walter K. Whigham*. Perhaps the decision to use steam power, in preference to diesels, was the best possible tribute to the skill and dedication of the shed staff. Closure came in June 1963 and the massive 1,400 tons coaling plant was demolished by explosives in spectacular fashion in 1964. This picture, taken on 16th September 1961, shows a general view of the depot premises with three A4s visible outside the 1862-built running shed. *R.C. Riley*

A Gresley-designed N2 Class 0-6-2T No. 69568 is seen near Hornsey on a sunny 20th September 1958, apparently hauling a train of empty main line stock. The locomotive was fitted with a small chimney and condensing apparatus for working over the Metropolitan Widened lines to Moorgate. The powerful N2s were built to the maximum Metropolitan lines loading gauge. These engines were a familiar sight on suburban and empty stock workings from Kings Cross for many years, until displaced by diesels. There were extensive carriage sidings at Hornsey, and also a steam motive power depot which is still used today, albeit for maintaining electric stock. *R.C. Riley*

A magnificent photograph of a magnificent locomotive, No. 60022 *Mallard* – what more need be said? The location is Oakleigh Park and this shot was taken in January 1963 during the particularly harsh winter of 1962/63. *A.G. Forsyth/Colour-Rail*

A few Great Northern Railway J6 Class 0-6-0s were allocated to Hornsey shed, but the class was much more common in the Peterborough, Doncaster, and Nottingham areas. So this shot is of particular interest, especially as the photographer was lucky enough to capture this example hauling a breakdown crane, which was presumably *en route* from Hornsey shed to a derailment. The locomotive is No. 64253, which was shedded at Hornsey for some years, and this picture was taken near Wood Green on 13th September 1958. Note the somewhat dilapidated breakdown vehicle, probably a tool van, which is formed immediately behind the locomotive. *R.C. Riley*

In steam days Hadley Wood was always a very popular photographic spot, which offered an open, clear view of passing trains, uncluttered by telegraph poles or other lineside structures. The attractive station buildings and trees beyond provided a splendid setting. In addition, northbound trains were climbing on a gradient of 1 in 200, which lasted for eight miles, from Wood Green to Potters Bar, so there was always a chance that a shot of a passing train would be enhanced by an impressive smoke effect. On this occasion the photographer was not rewarded with much smoke, but at least the sun was shining as A1 Pacific No. 60120 *Kittiwake* passed with a parcels train on the evening of 9th May 1963, just a few weeks before regular steam working ceased. Built in December 1948, *Kittiwake*, like most of its sister engines, had a tragically brief working life and was withdrawn in January 1964, eight months after this picture was taken. *Roy Hobbs*

The B1s were a very versatile design and could be observed on a wide range of duties from fast passenger trains to slow-moving freights. In addition, they had very generous route availability which greatly added to their usefulness. In this view, No. 61091 is depicted between Brookmans Park and Potters Bar on 18th June 1960, hauling an unidentified up passenger working which is comprised of BR Standard and Gresley designed coaches. The gradient at this point is slightly against southbound trains, Potters Bar Station being a summit in both directions. *C. Hogg*

Sir Nigel Gresley's V2 Class 2-6-2s were, without a doubt, one of his best and most successful designs. They were sometimes referred to as 'the engines that won the war', which was perhaps something of an exaggeration, but at least it indicated the regard in which they were held. Introduced in 1936, the V2s were a familiar sight on mixed traffic duties along the entire length of the East Coast Main Line for almost thirty years. The last active survivor was withdrawn from service in Scotland in December 1966. Here, a very presentable No. 60983 appears to be in a hurry as it sweeps around the curve north of Potters Bar with the down 'Scotch Goods', sometime in the late 1950s.
The late Derek Cross

BROAD STREET STATION

In the early 1860s the North London Railway was a very busy line, but its growth was restricted by the lack of convenient access to the City of London. A general meeting of shareholders held on 26th February 1861 agreed that an extension from Dalston Junction to Broad Street, on the edge of the City, would be desirable and an Act was obtained later that year. Construction of the Broad Street extension was extremely costly and involved the demolition of many properties, displacing 4,500 citizens. The LNWR was interested in a City goods depot and contributed to the cost of the line, which opened for passengers on 1st November 1865. Apart from a short-lived service to Wolverhampton prior to the First World War, Broad Street was always very much a suburban terminus, latterly being mainly served by electric services to Richmond and Watford. Steam traction survived on rush-hour trains into the 1960s however, and in this rare shot of steam at Broad Street, BR Standard Class 4MT No. 75031 is seen departing with the 6.05pm to Tring on an unknown date in the summer of 1962. *Michael Allen*

Class N7/5 No. 69663 leaves Liverpool Street with a train to Enfield Town on 4th October 1958, and begins the short 1 in 70 climb, mostly in a smoke-ridden and cavernous cutting, towards Bethnal Green. Note the economical design of the Gresley articulated stock, sharing a bogie between two carriages. These five-coach sets – known as 'Quint-Arts' – first appeared on the Enfield and Chingford services in the early 1920s, replacing elderly four wheeled carriages. At this time there was serious overcrowding on these services and a programme of track and signalling alterations was initiated, which resulted in the introduction of an improved, more intensive service – perhaps the busiest steam suburban service ever operated in Great Britain. The class of travel on the coaches was denoted by a colour code at door top level, thus earning these trains the title of 'Jazz Trains'. Amazingly, until the widespread introduction of N7s, the smaller J69 0-6-0Ts bore the brunt of these workings for a short period in the early 1920s. *R.C. Riley*

The location of this shot is readily identified by the station nameboard on the right of the picture. Class N7 No. 69728 is seen entering the station on 6th November 1960 with the 11.07am Liverpool Street to Enfield Town train, formed of one of the distinctive 'Quint-Art' sets. Bethnal Green Station had sawtooth platform canopies, which were so much beloved by the GER, and a common design feature of GER stations. *Michael Allen*

THE GREAT EASTERN LINES

A rather dirty B1 Class 4-6-0, No. 61252, passes Hackney Downs in charge of a Cambridge to Liverpool Street train on a sunny 27th August 1960. The coach immediately behind the locomotive is a Gresley-designed vehicle which contains a guard's brakevan. Note that the station's platform lighting appears to be undergoing modernisation! *Michael Allen*

A Locomotive Club of Great Britain railtour, hauled by D16/3 Class 4-4-0 No. 62613, passes through Seven Sisters Station on a glorious 12th July 1959. The ancestry of this elegant class can be traced back to 1900 when the pioneer 'Claud', the design of which was attributed to James Holden, entered service. It is thought, however, that much of the design work was undertaken by his assistant. The first one to be built was named after Claud Hamilton, then Chairman of the GER, hence the name 'Clauds'. No. 62613 was built at Stratford Works in 1923. The class was the mainstay of GER passenger services until the advent of the B12 4-6-0s, and could be regularly seen on Liverpool Street to Norwich expresses, which they worked with distinction. No. 62613 ended its days at March shed and could sometimes be observed working passenger trains on the Kings Lynn to Hunstanton line. Upon withdrawal in October 1960 No. 62613, which had become the last survivor of this celebrated class, was despatched to Stratford Works for breaking-up. This did not occur immediately however, and this gave rise to rumours that No. 62613 was to be preserved. Sadly, this speculation proved to be unfounded, so no representative of this famous class was saved for posterity. *C. Hogg/Colour-Rail*

The end of an era at Stratford shed occurred on 8th September 1962 when the depot closed to steam traction, an event which marked the virtual elimination of steam from the Great Eastern lines. Stratford shed had a long tradition of maintaining its engines in clean condition whenever possible, and was particularly renowned for the polished condition of its 'Britannias' and Liverpool Street pilot locomotives. It was, therefore, entirely appropriate that Stratford should rekindle a little of its old pride during the last weekend of steam, and three B1 Class 4-6-0s, which are seen here, were specially cleaned to mark the occasion. The following day No. 61156 worked a relief express from Harwich to Liverpool Street, and this is believed to have been the last scheduled steam passenger working on the GE Lines. Other locomotives present at Stratford shed on 8th September included J15s, J69s, N7s, and an Ivatt Class 2MT 2-6-0, but these were mostly out of steam at the rear of the shed. For a long period Stratford depot had the largest allocation of any shed in Great Britain and in 1937 this totalled no fewer than 492 engines, though it should be remembered that this figure included a large number of locomotives that were sub-shedded at various suburban depots. Following electrification of the North East London lines in November 1961 this total dwindled to a mere 56 engines. *Roy Hobbs*

Amongst the other locomotives visible at Stratford shed on the final day of steam was this vintage J15 0-6-0 No. 65465. These rugged and workmanlike engines were designed by T.W. Worsdell and introduced in 1883; construction continued until 1913, by which time a total of 289 engines had been built. They were originally designed for hauling goods trains, particularly coal from the Yorkshire coalfield down the GN&GE Joint line, and became numerically the largest class on the Great Eastern Railway. Their light axle loading made them versatile engines and especially useful for branch line work, for which the last 40 engines built were fitted with train brakes and screw couplings. No. 65465 began life as GER No. 567 at Stratford Works in March 1912 and survived until the end of steam on the GE Lines. *Roy Hobbs*

This everyday scene at North Woolwich shows N7 Class 0-6-2T No. 69682 waiting to leave with a train to Stratford (Low Level) on 28th June 1959. This design was originated by the GER and developed by the LNER to such effect that by 1928 more than 130 examples were in service. The class was primarily associated with the heavily-used suburban services from Liverpool Street, but members of the class could sometimes also be seen in other areas. The elegant structure in the background is North Woolwich Station building, which is deservedly a Grade II listed building. It dates from 1854 when it was built by the Eastern Counties Railway to replace an earlier wooden structure provided in 1847 for the opening of the line. Sadly, the building was derelict for a time, but ownership was transferred to a Trust which, with the assistance of the GER Society, successfully refurbished it and converted the building into a railway museum. The reopening ceremony was performed by Her Majesty The Queen Mother in 1984. *Michael Allen*

NORTH WOOLWICH TO PALACE GATES

N7 Class 0-6-2T No. 69692 is seen approaching North Woolwich with the 12.38pm from Stratford on 24th June 1961. The background is dominated by a very smart 'Routemaster' bus, RM 251, which was just over a year old when the picture was taken. Steam traction continued to haul rush hour services on this line until almost the end of steam on the GE Lines, and as late as 7th August 1962 an N7 Class engine was observed on the 4.50pm North Woolwich to Palace Gates train. *Michael Allen*

The 2¼ miles long branch from Seven Sisters to Palace Gates, opened throughout by the GER on 7th October 1878, was originally intended to connect with the GNR's Highgate to Alexandra Palace branch. The terminus at Palace Gates was built as a through station with the proposed extension in mind, but the line merely petered out in a goods yard and never reached the Palace. In 1929 the LNER laid in a connection with the Hertford Loop which was subsequently fully signalled and used by freight and excursion trains. By the early 1960s however, meagre rush-hours only services to North Woolwich were the sole services provided on the branch and even these ended when closure took place from 7th January 1963. The branch has subsequently been lifted, one of the few routes depicted in this book to suffer this fate. In this view, L1 Class 2-6-4T No. 67735 is seen making a smoky exit from the intermediate station of West Green with a Palace Gates-bound train in June 1962. *Roy Hobbs*

L1 Class No. 67729 stands in Palace Gates Station after arrival with an evening train from North Woolwich in September 1962. The Thompson L1s, which first appeared just before nationalisation, could hardly be described as one of their designer's most successful types. They suffered from heavy axlebox and motion wear which frequently caused a loud clanking noise and heralded their approach which could be heard from a considerable distance. Despite these deficiencies one hundred examples were constructed and they were a familiar sight on local trains on ER territory in the London area. A large number were rendered superfluous by electrification schemes, but eleven survived at Stratford until the end, mainly employed on humble duties, as seen here. *Roy Hobbs*

LONDON, TILBURY & SOUTHEND LINE

Few colour photographers were attracted by the Fenchurch Street to Shoeburyness line. They were undoubtedly deterred by the uninspiring nature of the route and the monotonous motive power, which generally consisted towards the end of steam of unappealing, dirty LMSR and BR-designed Class 4MT tank locomotives. So this is probably quite a rare colour view of Fenchurch Street Station in steam days. The engine depicted is Fairburn 2-6-4T No. 42679 which is awaiting departure with the 5.41pm to Tilbury Riverside on 11th April 1962. The origins of Fenchurch Street Station can be traced back to the 1830s when an extension of the London & Blackwall Railway from Minories to Fenchurch Street was sanctioned, and the new station, which was tucked away in a City side street, opened in August 1841. In 1934/35 the station was completely remodelled in an effort to cope with ever-increasing traffic. The line may not have been scenically attractive, but at least for many years it operated one of the most efficient and intensive steam suburban services in Great Britain. *Michael Allen*

A line of locomotives, all apparently stored out of use, stands at Plaistow shed in 1958: all appear to be either LTSR 0-6-2Ts or 4-4-2Ts. The engine nearest to the camera is No.41983, one of the former type, which was constructed by the North British Locomotive Company, Glasgow in 1903 (Works No.15753). One of a class of fourteen locomotives, it was originally LTSR No.70 and named *Hadleigh* and probably spent its entire career on the LTSR section. In LMSR days it was numbered 2223 and was later known as No.2183. No.41983 was withdrawn from service in February 1959. *E.V. Fry/Colour-Rail*

No.41969, also photographed at Plaistow shed, was a member of a class of 35 engines which was developed from the Whitelegg 79 Class, and first saw the light of day at Derby Works in 1930. It was numbered 2151 by the LMSR and later 1969. These engines were mostly confined to the LTSR section, but in about 1949 a small batch was surprisingly sent to Skipton in Yorkshire intended for use on local trains. The local enginemen would have nothing to do with them however, and the engines were moved to Carlisle for possible employment on stopping trains to Appleby. Once again the crews were unhappy, and it is thought that the locomotives were subsequently withdrawn in the mid-1950s without ever turning a wheel in the north of England. *E.V. Fry/Colour-Rail*

Various types of 2-6-4T locomotives worked on the Fenchurch Street line, but the most numerous were the Stanier-designed three cylinder engines, especially built for use on the LTSR line, which first appeared in 1934. Here, No. 42536 rolls into Barking with an eastbound Tilbury Line service on 18th March 1961. This engine was a product of Derby Works, being outshopped in December 1934, but by the time of this portrait it only had a further fifteen months of life remaining, being withdrawn in June 1962. At the time of this picture the track layout in the Barking area was undergoing drastic alterations prior to electrification. These included construction of fly-overs in order to reduce many of the conflicting movements which plagued operation of the station and also to facilitate cross-platform interchange between BR and LTE services. Part of one of these flyovers can just be discerned beyond the rear of the train. *Michael Allen*

Romantic Upminster! The author cannot recall any transparencies of BR steam at Upminster which have been published previously, so perhaps this picture may qualify as a 'World Exclusive'. This scene shows LMSR Fairburn 2-6-4T No. 42227 pausing with the 1.14pm Fenchurch Street to Shoeburyness train on 13th January 1962. The locomotive appears to be taking water, and readers will note the brazier, adjacent to the water crane, with its small supply of coal. At the time of this picture, some BR trains were already scheduled for electric operation during the off-peak periods, but full electric working did not take place until 17th June 1962. Besides being the terminus of the LTE District Line, the tracks of which are just discernible behind the platform fence, Upminster was also the junction for Tilbury to the south, and Romford to the north. It was therefore an important outer suburban interchange station, which justified stops by all LTSR trains, though there were a few exceptions to this rule. No. 42227 was one of a substantial batch of Fairburn tank engines allocated to the LTSR line. *Michael Allen*

In the late 1950s, before the start of cheap air travel, Victoria Station was still 'The Gateway to the Continent' for most travellers. Victoria had handled boat trains since the opening of the LCDR terminus, which was adjacent to the LBSCR station, in 1862, and from January 1920 all SECR boat trains ran from Victoria. It had a much lighter suburban service – not to mention better all round facilities – than either Charing Cross or Cannon Street. Apart from a small number of boat services to Newhaven which ran from the Central Section platforms, boat trains used the 'Chatham Side', which was graced by famous International expresses, such as the 'Golden Arrow' and the 'Night Ferry'. The romantic age of Continental travel has not been entirely eclipsed at Victoria however, because the 'Venice Simplon Orient Express', which is still steam-hauled on special occasions, is a regular sight in the terminus. In this photograph, taken on 2nd November 1957, two boat trains are apparently awaiting departure. On the left is BR Standard 'Britannia' Pacific No. 70014 *Iron Duke*, at the head of the 'Golden Arrow', while on the right is an unidentified service with Bulleid Light Pacific No. 34071 *601 Squadron*, in charge. Two 'Britannias' – the other was No. 70004 *William Shakespeare* – were based at Stewarts Lane shed at this time solely for use on the prestigious 'Golden Arrow', from Victoria to Dover Marine (later Western Docks). *C. Hogg*

SOUTHERN REGION – EASTERN SECTION

In steam days, most photographers were understandably drawn to the main London termini and principal routes radiating from the Capital, so consequently colour transparencies of everyday, unglamorous workings on less prominent routes are comparatively rare. The author was, therefore, especially pleased when this picture, which was taken from the sliding front window of the signal box at Nunhead, was submitted. The train is the 3.50pm empty stock working from Rotherhithe Road to Cannon Street, which presumably had to reverse at both Blackheath and Blackfriars before reaching its destination. The coaches later formed a down rush-hour train to the Kent Coast. Motive power is provided by a rather unkempt BR Standard 2-6-2T No. 84023. The train is travelling over the route of the erstwhile Nunhead to Greenwich Park branch. This had lain derelict since closure in 1917, but in 1929 a connection was laid from the dormant Greenwich Park line to Lewisham Station, and a further curve was laid which connected the Mid-Kent Line with the main SECR London to Tonbridge line. These new sections of line enabled transfer freight trains bound for Hither Green to avoid the congested tracks through London Bridge. The line from Nunhead to Lewisham was thus given a new lease of life, and in 1935 was electrified for use by rush hour passenger services from Holborn Viaduct and Blackfriars to the Dartford lines. *Paul Leavens*

In the picture on the left, the 'Golden Arrow' boat train leaves Victoria, and climbs the short 1 in 62 incline to Grosvenor Bridge on a sunny morning sometime in the early 1960s. An immaculately turned out rebuilt Bulleid Pacific No. 34100, *Appledore*, is in charge. Note the down 'Brighton Belle' is running parallel on an adjacent track. During this period both trains left Victoria at 11.00am, so a lucky photographer could obtain a rare shot of two Pullman Car trains in the same picture, as seen here. The 'Golden Arrow' was inaugurated on 15th May 1929, but the pre-war train was not a great success because its introduction coincided with the world economic recession which badly affected patronage. It ceased operation at the start of the Second World War. After the end of hostilities the 'Golden Arrow' was reintroduced on 15th April 1946, leaving London at 10.00am and arriving in Paris at 6.45pm. Over the years, various changes were made to the timings to increase custom and fight off stiff competition from the airlines. In June 1961 the train was steam-hauled for the last time, and it disappeared from the timetable in 1972 – coincidentally the last year of operation of the 'Brighton Belle'. *C. Hogg*

'King Arthur' Class 4-6-0 No. 30796 *Sir Dodinas Le Savage* leaves Cannon Street with an unidentified express, presumably bound for the Kent Coast, on 31st May 1958. The train is composed of Maunsell-designed corridor coaches. Cannon Street opened on 1st September 1866 as the City station of the South Eastern Railway, and was noted for its distinctive train shed and prominent towers, considerable landmarks which jutted out across the north bank of the River Thames. The arched roof, which suffered wartime damage that prevented it from being reglazed, was removed shortly after this picture was taken. Being located in the heart of the City of London, Cannon Street Station has always been extremely busy during the peak hours. There was, however, little traffic at other times of the day, and particularly at weekends, with the result that it was closed after Saturday lunchtime until early the following Monday morning. Latterly, of course, with the general loss of Saturday office working it lost all of its Saturday services. *R.C. Riley*

The most striking difference between this illustration and the previous picture is, of course, the fact that the overall roof has disappeared. Removal of the roof commenced in 1958 and by January 1959 it had been completely dismantled. The walls and towers were retained following representations from leading academics and architects, but some people said they looked rather meaningless without the graceful, unifying curve of the station's roof. The demolition of the roof marked the end of an era at Cannon Street Station, and another era ended there when steam traction on Ramsgate services bowed out during the weekend of 13th/14th June 1959, which marked the start of the summer timetable. Here Bulleid Pacific No. 34004 *Yeovil* is seen departing with one of the final steam-hauled commuter services, the 5.44pm to Ramsgate, on Friday 12th June 1959. Judging by the 'streamers' (thoughtfully provided by BR free of charge!), some commuters appear to be celebrating the demise of 'old fashioned' steam traction, or perhaps enthusiasts were enjoying a last run prior to electric traction taking over. No. 34004 was destined to survive the end of SR steam, hauling express trains on the Waterloo to Weymouth line. *R.C. Riley*

Bathed in glorious early morning sunshine, SECR E1 Class 4-4-0 No. 31507 approaches New Cross Station in charge of the 7.24am London Bridge to Ramsgate train, which was routed via Tonbridge, Ashford and Dover. This train was the last booked duty for an SECR 4-4-0 and was frequently patronised by enthusiasts. This portrait was taken in June 1961, just a few days before Phase II of the Kent Coast Lines Electrification Scheme was inaugurated which resulted in the elimination of steam traction from most routes, and put paid to such evocative scenes. No. 31507 was built as an E Class locomotive in September 1908 at Ashford Works, but was rebuilt by Maunsell in 1920 and reclassified E1. Sadly, the working days of this fine old engine were almost over, and it was withdrawn during the following month and broken up, with almost indecent haste, at Ashford Works at the end of August 1961. *Paul Leavens*

When the LCDR and SER amalgamated to form the SECR in 1899, Harry Wainwright took over the new position of Locomotive & Carriage Superintendent. One of his first tasks was to oversee the design of a new standard goods engine, and the outcome was the C Class, which was based on the LCDR B Class. The new locomotives were an immediate success and eventually 109 were constructed, including some by outside contractors, though the bulk were built at Ashford Works. In service they were simple, robust and reliable machines with a good turn of speed. Indeed, they were such good performers that they were frequently pressed into service on seaside excursions and local passenger workings. Almost the entire class entered BR ownership in 1948, and in 1960 a total of 60 still remained in use. By 1964, the class had been reduced to three survivors, appropriately employed as works shunters at Ashford, and one of those was later saved for preservation on the Bluebell Railway. In this view Hither Green-based No. 31690, a Neilson Reid & Co. product of July 1900, is depicted leaving the down sidings at Grove Park with the 8.05am empty coaching stock train to Charing Cross in March 1960. The coaches would later form a train to Ashford and Dover.
Paul Leavens

Judging by the predominantly cloudy sky, the photographer appears to have been very lucky to photograph Maunsell N Class 2-6-0 No. 31854 with the sun shining, just after passing Shortlands junction with an unidentified up train on 3rd August 1958. The coaches, like the locomotive, are also of Maunsell design. At this time, extensive track improvements were being undertaken in the area preparatory to the inauguration of Phase One of the Kent Coast electrification in June 1959, hence the new track in the foreground. No. 31854 was one of 50 N Class engines assembled at Ashford Works from parts supplied by Woolwich Arsenal, except for the boilers which were the work of the North British Locomotive Co. It first saw the light of day in March 1925. *R.C. Riley*

An unidentified up boat train, hauled by unrebuilt 'Merchant Navy' Pacific No. 35001 *Channel Packet*, was photographed near Bromley South in April 1959. These Bulleid-designed locomotives were amongst the most interesting, and certainly the most unconventional, ever to run in Great Britain. At this time Nos. 35001 and 35028 *Clan Line* (which was also still in original condition) were allocated to Stewarts Lane shed for passenger duties on the South Eastern Section, and both remained there until Phase One of the Kent Coast Electrification Scheme was implemented in June 1959. During this period, a rebuilt 'Merchant Navy', No. 35015 *Rotterdam Lloyd* was also based at Stewarts Lane shed. In June, they were all transferred to the Western Section for use on express passenger duties from Waterloo. It is likely that *Channel Packet*, which was outshopped from Eastleigh Works in August 1959 in modified form, was rebuilt prior to entering traffic on the Western Section. It ran for just over five years in modified condition before being withdrawn in November 1964. *The late Derek Cross*

SOUTHERN REGION – CENTRAL SECTION

A general view of the Central Section platforms at London Bridge Station on 14th May 1959. LBSCR E4 Class 0-6-2T No. 32474 is busy shunting what appears to be a van train. London's first passenger-carrying railway was opened by the London & Greenwich Railway between Spa Road and Deptford on 8th February 1836, so it could be said that Spa Road was London's first terminus. That station was a purely temporary affair however, and ten months later, on 14th December 1836, the station at London Bridge was formally opened by the Lord Mayor of London. In June 1839 the London & Croydon Railway (which later formed part of the LBSCR) opened for business and for a time shared London Bridge Station. In 1850 however, the LBSCR decided to build its own station approximately on the site seen here. *R.C. Riley*

BR Standard Class 4MT 2-6-4T No. 80141 poses at London Bridge before departure with the 5.20pm to Tunbridge Wells West via the Oxted line, on 21st August 1962. Originally a continental goods depot occupied this area, but this was closed in 1899 and four new platforms constructed on the site. These were opened in 1902, together with a new footbridge connecting them to the high level platforms. At the time of this picture steam traction was still dominant on Oxted Line workings from London Bridge, but the introduction of BRCW Type 3 (later Class 33) diesel locomotives and diesel units on such diagrams in May 1963 led to the rapid elimination of steam traction. Within a few months, the steam diagrams had been decimated by the diesel infiltrators to such an extent that only a handful of steam workings to and from London survived. One of the last trains to be regularly steam-hauled was the 5.06pm SX Tunbridge Wells West to London Bridge. The last reported booked steam workings from London Bridge occurred on 4th January 1964 when Bulleid Light Pacific No. 34070 *Manston* took the 3.27am newspaper train to Eastbourne, and Maunsell 'Mogul' No. 31827 powered the 4.50am to Tonbridge via Redhill. *Michael Allen*

In the picture on the right, Maunsell 'Schools' 4-4-0 No. 30911 *Dover*, in quite reasonable external condition, climbs the stiff 1 in 100 gradient between Brockley and Honor Oak Park stations on 1st June 1962. The train is the celebrated 5.25pm commuter working from London Bridge to Reading and Tonbridge, which is comprised, as might be expected, of two sets of stock. The Reading portion is formed largely of Bulleid-designed vehicles plus one BR Standard coach, while the Tonbridge section appears to be made up of all Maunsell carriages. What a wonderful way to commute to and from work – in spacious main line stock, steam hauled, with about 'ten on'! Sadly, this was the last year of operation of the 'Schools' Class locomotives, which were widely regarded as Richard Maunsell's most outstanding design, capable of prodigious feats of haulage out of all proportion to their modest size. No. 30911 was reportedly the last active 'Schools' Class locomotive on the Central Division. It worked the 7.27am Reading to London Bridge train (the inward working of the train seen here) on 28th December 1962, and instead of returning to Reading it was sent down to Brighton on the 4.40pm from London Bridge, which was routed via the Oxted Line. That was *Dover*'s last working, because on the following day it was unceremoniously despatched to a dump of withdrawn engines in Hove goods yard, and broken-up for scrap at Eastleigh Works in September 1963. *C. Hogg*

A beautiful picture of a most elegant engine. LBSCR H2 Class 'Atlantic' No. 32424 *Beachy Head* is depicted at Norwood Junction shed on 12th April 1958, prior to working the 'Sussex Coast Limited' railtour on the following day. This special train, which ran from Victoria to Newhaven and returned to London from Brighton, was run to commemorate the end of the LBSCR 'Atlantics'. *Beachy Head* was appropriately employed on the down run to Newhaven, the class having been closely associated with the Victoria to Newhaven boat trains for many years. During the journey the veteran No. 32424 achieved a creditable maximum speed of 70mph crossing the Ouse Valley viaduct, north of Haywards Heath. *Beachy Head* was withdrawn from service almost immediately following this assignment and, sadly, was cut-up for scrap at Eastleigh Works within a few weeks. Steam enthusiasts still mourn the loss of this magnificent locomotive, which was destroyed shortly before the preservation movement became established. *R. C. Riley*

A grimy Maunsell 'Schools' class 4-4-0 No. 30930 *Radley* coasts downhill through Norwood Junction with the 5.25pm London Bridge to Reading and Tonbridge train on 10th August 1962. This was not a particularly glamorous location, and is unlikely to have been widely photographed in colour. No. 30930 was constructed at Eastleigh Works in December 1934 and was initially allocated to Fratton shed for use on the Waterloo to Portsmouth expresses. It later operated from Bournemouth shed, but in 1946 *Radley* was moved to Brighton and by 1949 had migrated to Bricklayers Arms. No. 30930 then worked from a variety of sheds, and was still in traffic at the end of 1962 when all of the surviving 'Schools' Class locomotives were withdrawn, apparently as a result of an accountancy move aimed at reducing the number of steam engines inherited by the British Railways Board. The origins of the 5.25pm business train from London Bridge, which was the last regular steam train between London and Redhill, can be traced back to pre-grouping days, but the train's ancestry obviously failed to impress the BR operating authorities of the day who withdrew it at very short notice on 18th February 1963, apparently because engine crews were required for freight work. It was replaced by an electric unit running between London Bridge and Redhill, where connecting steam trains were provided for Reading and Tonbridge passengers. *Michael Allen*

This panoramic view of Crystal Palace (Low Level) Station shows LBSCR C2X Class 0-6-0 No. 32543 leaving at the head of a ramblers' special on 3rd June 1956. The train is heading in a north-easterly direction, towards the junction with the East Croydon to London Bridge line at Sydenham. The very large and ornamented station buildings, in the background, were built to cater for the excursion traffic to the Crystal Palace, but this was destroyed by fire in 1936. This picture was presumably taken at a weekend, hence there are three trains of 4-SUB electric units, all complete with the regulation tail lamp, berthed in sidings in the station area. The first railway to reach Crystal Palace was floated in 1853 by the West End of London and Crystal Palace Railway, which obtained powers for a line connecting the LSWR at (what later became) Clapham Junction with an LBSCR spur from Sydenham. An extension to Norwood was later authorised, and this route was the LBSCR's principal line into the West End of London, until the Windmill Bridge Junction (Croydon) to Balham section was opened in 1862. *R.C. Riley*

The train on the facing page may have the unmistakable appearance of a railtour, but appearances can sometimes deceive! It was, in fact, a ramblers' special from Greenford to Horsted Keynes and Ardingly, which was recorded near Selsdon on 11th May 1958. Despite the picture of a bluebell on the headboard, the train had no connection with the Bluebell Railway Preservation Society, which had not been formed by this date. The train had been hauled as far as East Croydon by the record breaking GWR 4-4-0 No. 3440 *City of Truro*, but the SR operating authorities had placed an embargo on it proceeding any further south, hence the appearance of this indigenous and immaculately turned-out LBSCR K Class Mogul No. 32342. Later on during its journey the special traversed the dormant East Grinstead to Horsted Keynes section of the line to Lewes (the 'Bluebell Line'), which had recently been closed to traffic. Fortunately, the dormant stretch was being retained by BR on a 'care and maintenance' basis and remained open for limited use. If the Bluebell Railway's plans come to fruition, it will again be possible to travel by rail from London to Horsted Keynes (and on to Sheffield Park!), but sadly the motive power cannot be repeated, because none of these distinctive K Class engines survived into preservation. *R.C. Riley*

The traditional Royal Train from Victoria to Tattenham Corner, conveying HM The Queen and HRH The Duke of Edinburgh to the Derby Day race meeting on Epsom Downs, passes East Croydon on Wednesday 6th June 1962. Motive power was provided by Stewarts Lane depot in the shape of 'Schools' Class 4-4-0 No. 30926 *Repton*. This is in absolutely magnificent external condition, complete with burnished buffers and running with the special 'Royal' locomotive headcode. It is still possible to photograph the Royal Derby Day 'special' at this location, albeit with electric traction, but the background would be much different today. Apart from the brick retaining walls – which still have the recesses for the overhead a.c. electrification girders – virtually everything else in the picture has changed beyond recognition. Nearly all of the older buildings have since disappeared, including those of East Croydon Station, which are located on the roadbridge. The tall Essex House office block on the left, which housed the SR Central Section Manager's Offices and was built as recently as 1961, has also gone, and even the track layout has been changed following radical alterations in the early 1980s. The tracks to the old Croydon Central Station used to branch off to the left, across the ground occupied by the building site (for a multi-storey car park) in the picture. *Mike Hudson*

On the glorious autumn afternoon of 2nd October 1961, BR Standard Class 4MT tank locomotive No. 80018 enters Riddlesdown Station in charge of the 3.08pm Victoria to Tunbridge Wells West train. The locomotive has been 'shut off' and the train appears to be coasting before stopping at the station, so the stiff 1 in 100 gradient which applies at this point is hardly discernible. In fact, between East Croydon and Hurst Green Junction, where the train would diverge from the East Grinstead line, there is barely a half a mile of level track, so this route across the North Downs was always a stern test for enginemen. *Paul Leavens*

An LMSR-designed Class 4MT 2-6-4T locomotive, No. 42070, heads a Tunbridge Wells West bound passenger train across Riddlesdown Viaduct with the sun on the side in September 1959. Note the two vintage non-corridor coaches formed immediately behind the locomotive. These Fairburn tank engines were designed during the dying days of the LMSR, and the majority were constructed under BR auspices. No. 42070 was amongst a batch of 41 engines built at Brighton Works specifically to replace ageing LBSCR passenger engines on the Central Section. It emerged from Brighton Works in November 1950 and was employed on the SR until all of the Central Section's Fairburn locomotives were exchanged for BR Standard engines in early 1960. It worked elsewhere on BR before being withdrawn in June 1965. *The late Derek Cross*

Industrial Croydon! In a scene more reminiscent of the industrial north of England, a W Class 2-6-4T No.31919 was photographed passing Waddon Marsh, on the Wimbledon to West Croydon line, with the 10.30am coal empties from Croydon 'B' power station sidings to Norwood Yard in May 1959. The power station's cooling towers can be seen in the left background behind the retort buildings of Croydon gas works. The train was travelling along a short freight-only line which formed a second running line serving industrial installations in the Beddington Lane and Waddon Marsh areas. Also on the left, stands an Andrew Barclay 0-6-0ST *Moss Bay* shunting coke wagons from the retort house. It is difficult to believe that this picture was taken only about a mile from the heart of Croydon which, even at that time, was a go-ahead, bustling shopping and commercial centre for a large area of south London. This interesting line through Waddon Marsh was opened in 1855 by the Wimbledon & Croydon Company and leased to the LBSCR during the following year. The line was electrified in 1930, and although it served a predominantly suburban area, the route had a curiously rural atmosphere, with some stretches being single (electrified) track, as seen here. In addition, the signalmen at two intermediate stations issued tickets from their signal boxes! Today, the route is no longer part of the National system and, at the time of writing, is undergoing a radical transformation as a section of Croydon's new tramway system. *Paul Leavens*

Electrification (on the third-rail system) of most routes in south London took place under Southern Railway auspices in the late 1920s and 1930s, with the result that steam workings on some of these lines became very much a rarity, except on freight and departmental duties. After that time, Epsom was hardly a rewarding location for the steam aficionado, and consequently few colour photographs, or indeed pictures of steam traction of any description, were taken in the area. In this interesting picture an unidentified Bulleid Q1 Class 0-6-0 is depicted at Epsom Goods at the head of a Civil Engineer's Dept. train during relaying operations on Sunday 18th September 1955. All of the railway installations in this picture, except the main running lines, have since been obliterated by housing development. *Neil Davenport*

Surprisingly, very few transparencies of steam trains in action between Victoria and East Croydon were submitted for inclusion in this album. Perhaps with the amount of activity on the South Western Section, the Central Section lines tended to be overlooked by photographers. Here, a BR Standard 2-6-4T No.80137 is seen awaiting departure from Clapham Junction with the 1.08pm Victoria to Tunbridge Wells West train on 25th September 1960. Note the vintage station nameboard. *Michael Allen*

Waterloo Station, immortalised in the prize-winning British Transport Film Unit documentary *Terminus*, was for many years, until the reconstruction of Euston, the only London terminus to be built in the twentieth century. The forerunner of Waterloo was Nine Elms Station, which was opened by the London & Southampton Railway (later the LSWR) in May 1838, but it soon became clear that Nine Elms was hardly a convenient location for local passenger traffic into the Capital. An extension to a 'West End' location was approved, the new station at Waterloo opening in July 1848. A further extension to London Bridge was also proposed, but this was later abandoned. During the ensuing years Waterloo was extended in a haphazard fashion, and became a confused jumble of buildings in which the unwary traveller could easily get lost. In the year 1900 the LSWR embarked on a long overdue rebuilding project, but the First World War intervened and the new station was not fully operational until 1922. Pictures taken inside Waterloo Station are not plentiful, so this shot is of particular interest. The locomotive depicted is restored LSWR T9 Class No. 120 (formerly BR No. 30120) which is seen awaiting departure with a Basingstoke-bound train in July 1962. This graceful and very distinctive engine was scheduled for preservation by the former British Transport Commission and had been restored to LSWR livery at Eastleigh Works. It was employed in regular service for some time after restoration however, before being officially retired. At the time of writing it can be seen on the Bluebell Railway, though it is not currently operational. *Roy Hobbs*

SOUTHERN REGION – WESTERN SECTION

LSWR Urie-designed S15 Class 4-6-0 No. 30497 basks in the sunshine at Waterloo before departing with the 11.54am semi-fast train to Basingstoke on 1st September 1962. Locomotives of this class were built in various batches from 1920 to 1936, and some of the later Maunsell-designed locomotives were built with six-wheel tenders, specifically for use on the Central Section. Fortunately, representatives of both these variants have survived into preservation. *Neville Simms*

Nine Elms will always be fondly remembered as London's last BR steam shed, or 'motive power depot' to quote its official title. In this portrait four Bulleid 'Pacifics' are seen 'on shed' on 1st July 1966. They are (left to right) Nos 35023 *Holland-Afrika Line*, 34019 *Bideford*, 35013 *Blue Funnel* and 34002 *Salisbury*. At the turn of the century the shed had about 200 engines on its books, a figure that had been halved by the end of the 1950s. When the shed closed in July 1967 it could only muster an allocation of 24 locomotives, which must have been lost in such an extensive site. Towards the end, many of the engines were in appalling mechanical condition, and there are stories of footplatemen regularly 'failing' their allocated locomotive due to a leaking firebox or similar defect, and often the replacement engine was also rejected. In addition to the wretched state of the motive power, there were few tools in the stores, and a shortage of enginemen's footplate equipment meant that the tools frequently 'disappeared' if not kept under lock and key. Needless to say, the official complement of 25 engine cleaners was purely theoretical, to which the disgraceful, grime-encrusted exteriors of the locomotive fleet bore ample testament. Despite, or perhaps because of, the neglected and filthy state of the buildings and steam dinosaurs they housed, Nine Elms caught the imagination of film makers and artists. Paul Barnes captured the sights and sounds on film and David Shepherd – who took up residence at the shed during its dying days – immortalised the glory, gloom and squalor of Nine Elms on canvas. So, Nine Elms shed, where BR steam traction made its last stand in London, will never be forgotten. *Paul Leavens*

Maunsell 'Lord Nelson' Class No. 30865 *Sir John Hawkins* passes Queen's Road (Battersea) Station with an unidentified down train, possibly, judging by the headcode disc, a Waterloo to Southampton Docks boat train. This picture was taken on 26th July 1959. The two coaches immediately behind the locomotive are BR Standard vehicles in the distinctive carmine and cream livery, which was in vogue on BR at that time. No. 30865 was the final member of its class to be constructed, being outshopped from Eastleigh Works in November 1929. It was destined to have the shortest career of all the 'Lord Nelsons', becoming the first to be withdrawn from traffic, in May 1961. *R.C. Riley*

In the late 1950s a small contingent of WR 0-6-0PT locomotives was transferred to Nine Elms shed for use on empty stock workings between Waterloo and Clapham Yard. In this illustration, taken on 25th September 1960, No. 9770 is seen approaching Clapham Yard at the head of what appears to be an extremely long rake of Bulleid coaching stock. These engines were not in sole charge of these duties however, because a number of LSWR M7 Class 0-4-4Ts, which were more 'traditional' power on these workings, were still working from Nine Elms at this time. Another group of these pannier tank engines could be found at Folkestone, where they replaced R1 Class 0-6-0Ts on banking duties on the very steeply-graded Harbour branch. *Michael Allen*

In this scene, 'Merchant Navy' Class Pacific No. 35015 *Rotterdam Lloyd* is seen at the approaches to Clapham Yard in April 1961. Locomotives of the calibre of No. 35015 were more usually to be seen speeding through Clapham Junction Station at the head of a prestigious, named express rather than engaged on mundane empty stock duty, as seen here. The sight of an express passenger locomotive on an empty stock working at Clapham Junction was not as unusual as might be supposed however, because there were booked turns for Pacifics which involved such work. In most cases the engine would have been used following its arrival at Waterloo with a passenger train, and would have retired to Nine Elms for servicing after reaching Clapham Yard. This locomotive had a particularly interesting history, being one of the three unrebuilt 'Merchant Navy' Class engines based at Stewarts Lane shed during the late 1950s. This was a result of a deliberate policy of concentrating the rebuilt members of the class on the South Western Section, where the duties were more demanding. In June 1958 it became the first of the trio to be rebuilt, the other two being similarly dealt with during 1959. Mysteriously, No. 35015 reappeared on the South Eastern Section following rebuilding and became the only rebuilt example of its class to be allocated to that section. On 16th May 1959 it powered the 11.00am Victoria to Dover Marine boat train, but was reallocated to Nine Elms the following month. In February 1964 it fell victim to a decision to cease general repairs on the class and was consequently withdrawn from service, being one of the first to go for scrap. *Paul Leavens*

The 'Bournemouth Belle' was undoubtedly one of the most luxurious and famous trains to serve London. The 'Belle' was inaugurated on Sunday 5th July 1931 and, despite the economic recession which prevailed at that time, achieved a high level of patronage. Initially a portion ran through to Weymouth, but this proved to be loss-making and was quickly withdrawn. For the first few years the train ran daily during the summer period only, but operated on every Sunday throughout the year. When more prosperous times arrived, daily running all-year-round was authorised and this commenced on 1st January 1936. Usual motive power was a 'Lord Nelson' Class 4-6-0, but 'King Arthurs' sometimes deputised. During the Second World War all the Pullman Cars were mothballed, but the train soon reappeared after the end of hostilities, but with a startling change in its motive power. Bulleid 'Merchant Navy' Class Pacifics, with their distinctive air-smoothed casing, were by this time rostered. During the period of post-war austerity passengers taking a relaxing trip on the 'Belle' could forget, at least for a couple of hours, bread rationing and other deprivations. By the late 1950s the 'Belle' had become an extremely heavy formation, sometimes consisting of as many as twelve 12-wheeled Pullman Cars, weighing more than 500 tons. Apart from a brief flirtation with diesel haulage in the early 1950s, the opulent 'Belle' was steam-worked almost to the end. Brush Type 4 diesels took over in January 1967, just before the train was withdrawn in July of the same year. What a pity that the unimaginative SR management of the time would not permit a gleaming (or even a dirty!) 'Merchant Navy' to work the last 'Belle', thus allowing SR steam to die with a flourish. What a magnificent, and memorable sight that would have been! The down 'Belle' is seen near Clapham Junction on 13th September 1959 with No. 35001 *Channel Packet* in charge. *R.C. Riley*

Durnsford Road power station, with its famous chimneys which were a landmark for many miles around, provides an unmistakable setting for this picture of H15 Class 4-6-0 No. 30491 pulling the 12.39pm Waterloo to Basingstoke semi-fast train on 20th August 1960. The train is mainly comprised of coaches of Bulleid design, except for the vehicle immediately behind the engine which is from the Maunsell era. Note the van on the rear. Wimbledon Park berthing sidings are partially visible on the left of the picture. In the background an electric train can be seen heading along the down slow line towards Wimbledon Station. This scene has changed out of all recognition because, following demolition of the power station, a modern maintenance depot for electric stock was constructed on the site. *C. Hogg*

Towards the end of SR steam the condition of many engines was, as previously stated, quite appalling. It is a wonder that the locomotives kept going at all, bearing in mind the policy of 'minimum expenditure' on the steam fleet which prevailed at the time. In this picture however, Bulleid 'West Country' Pacific No. 34013 *Okehampton* seems to be in quite reasonable fettle, as it passes Wimbledon with a down Bournemouth Line express on the sunny afternoon of 11th March 1967. Most unusually for that period, it appears to have its nameplates still intact. Note that the train is formed of a mixture of Bulleid and BR Standard coaches, with one of the latter vehicles in blue and grey livery. The suburban line to Mitcham Junction and West Croydon can be seen diverging in the far background, behind the locomotive. *David Clark*

It is always interesting to see pictures of preserved locomotives when in BR service, and here BR Standard 4-6-0 No. 73082 *Camelot* (currently on the Bluebell Railway) is depicted hauling an up van train past Weybridge in June 1962. The ex-works coach in the formation suggests that the train originated at Eastleigh. Locomotives of this class were prominent on Bournemouth Line passenger duties right up to the end of steam working, though they tended to be used on the less onerous duties. No. 73082 was one of a class of 172 engines built between 1951 and 1957. Construction was shared between Derby and Doncaster works, with the former establishment having the lion's share. *Camelot* was a Derby-built example, and was turned-out in June 1955. It spent its entire working life on the Southern Region, being initially based at Stewarts Lane for haulage of Kent Coast expresses and boat trains from Victoria. In 1959, following inauguration of Phase One of the Kent Coast electrification, No. 73082 migrated 'up the road' to nearby Nine Elms shed, for use on services from Waterloo. After a brief working career *Camelot* was withdrawn from service on 19th June 1966, and despatched to Woodham's Yard at Barry, in South Wales. But hope remained, because No. 73082 was not broken-up, and a society was formed with the object of saving the engine for posterity. *Camelot* eventually arrived on the Bluebell Line in October 1979 and returned to steam, following a protracted and painstaking restoration, in October 1995. *Geoff Rixon*

THE WEST LONDON LINE

During the 1960s, the West London Line carried a wide range of traffic, but perhaps the best known workings were the two weekday return rush-hour trips which ran between Clapham Junction and Kensington Olympia. These trains were unadvertised, and ran mainly for the benefit of Post Office workers, but they were steam-hauled, so naturally the timings were well-known to the steam enthusiast fraternity who frequently patronised them. In this view of Kensington Olympia taken in October 1962, SECR H Class 0-4-4T No.31305 is seen shunting its stock prior to hauling an evening train to Clapham Junction. The train is formed of BR Standard non-corridor stock, except for the brake coach, which is of Maunsell design. Note the advertisement for the now long-defunct London 'Evening News'. *Roy Hobbs*

The West London Line continued to be used by scheduled seasonal holiday trains until the mid-1960s, when this traffic was killed off by the growth in private car ownership and the increasing popularity of overseas package holidays. In addition, there was intense pressure on the railway authorities to reduce the operating deficit, which was increasing alarmingly at this time. This type of seasonal holiday working, for which sets of little-used rolling stock were retained throughout the year, was seen as being uneconomic, and quickly disappeared from the timetables. Here, the 10.47am SO train from Walsall to Hastings passes through Kensington Olympia on the down through line behind Bulleid 'Battle of Britain' Class Pacific No. 34057 *Biggin Hill* on 27th July 1963. This train also served Brighton and Eastbourne, where reversals were necessary before reaching Hastings, its ultimate destination, so Hastings-bound passengers still had 2fi hours of travelling ahead of them – but at least (in the author's opinion!) they had the compensation of being steam hauled! *Michael Allen*

The West London Line was opened in two sections, the first stretch from a junction with the LNWR near Kensal Green to the Kensington canal basin at Warwick Road, being opened by the West London Railway in May 1844. This line ran through a district which, at that time, was open countryside and consequently it was very little used. Its fortunes improved, however, when the West London Extension Railway, jointly promoted by various companies, extended the line southwards to Clapham Junction and Longhedge, Battersea. This now provided a valuable cross-London link from the north to the vast network of lines south of the River Thames. This section was opened to traffic on 1st August 1863. After the Second World War, with the advent of more generous holidays, the route was heavily used by inter-regional holiday trains during the summer months, and one of these is shown here. The train is a Saturdays only 'extra' from Hastings to Manchester conveying homegoing holiday-makers, which is depicted leaving Kensington Olympia Station behind LMSR 'Black Five' No. 45426 on 22nd August 1959. The summer of that year was generally very warm and sunny, so although the passengers were no doubt sad to be returning home, hopefully they would at least be taking some happy memories back with them. *R.C. Riley*